# Worship Band Play-Along

## VOCAL EDITION *Volume 2*

# Here I Am to Worship

Recorded and produced by Jim Reith at BeatHouse Music, Milwaukee, WI

Lead Vocals by Tonia Emrich and Jim Reith
Background Vocals by Jim Reith, Janna Wolf and Joy Palisoc Bach
Guitars by Mike DeRose and Joe Gorman
Bass by Chris Kringel
Keyboard by Kurt Cowling
Drums by Del Bennett

ISBN 978-1-4234-1716-3

## HAL•LEONARD® CORPORATION

7777 W. BLUEMOUND RD. P.O. BOX 13819 MILWAUKEE, WI 53213

Visit Hal Leonard Online at
**www.halleonard.com**

# Come, Now Is the Time to Time to Worship

**Words and Music by Brian Doerksen**

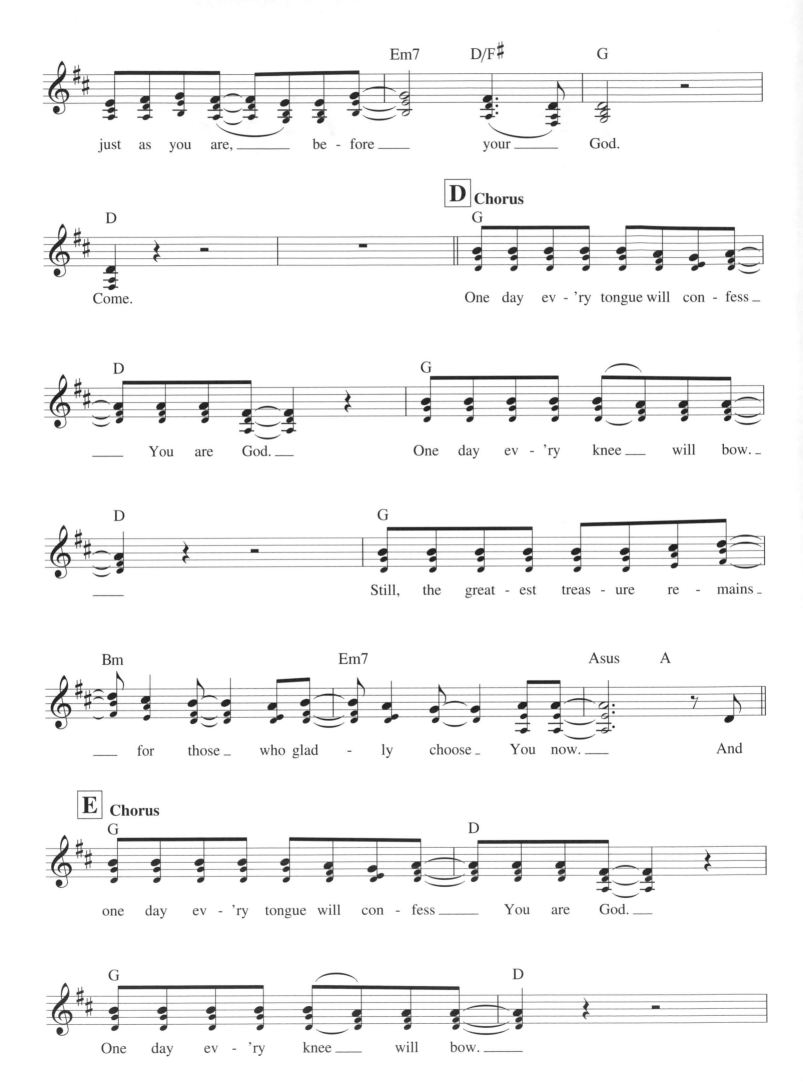

just as you are, _____ be - fore _____ your _____ God.

**D** Chorus

Come. One day ev - 'ry tongue will con - fess _____

_____ You are God. _____ One day ev - 'ry knee _____ will bow. _____

_____ Still, the great - est treas - ure re - mains _____

_____ for those _____ who glad - ly choose _____ You now. _____ And

**E** Chorus

one day ev - 'ry tongue will con - fess _____ You are God. _____

One day ev - 'ry knee _____ will bow. _____

# Give Us Clean Hands

Words and Music by Charlie Hall

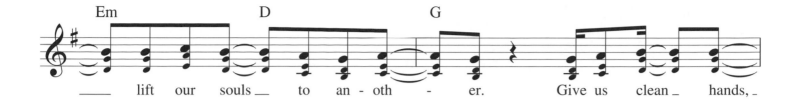

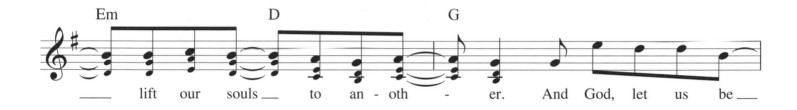

9

# Hear Our Praises

**Words and Music by Reuben Morgan**

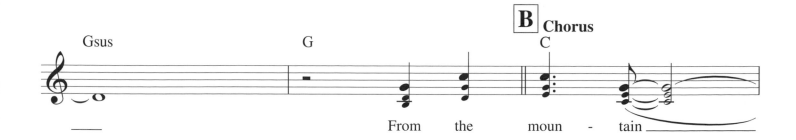

From the moun - tain

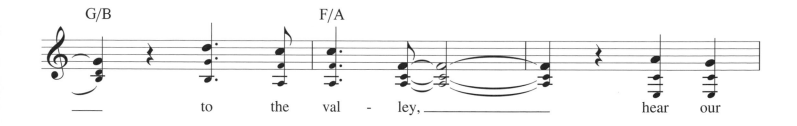

to the val - ley, _____ hear our

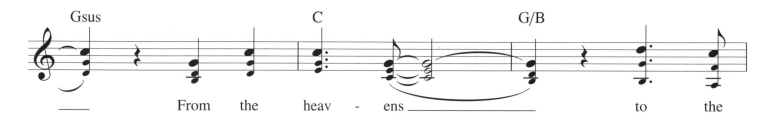

prais - es _____ rise to You. _____

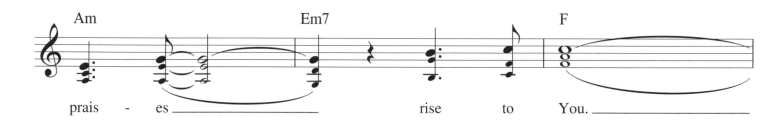

From the heav - ens _____ to the

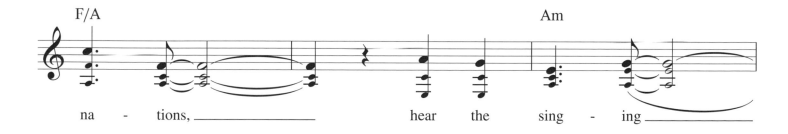

na - tions, _____ hear the sing - ing _____

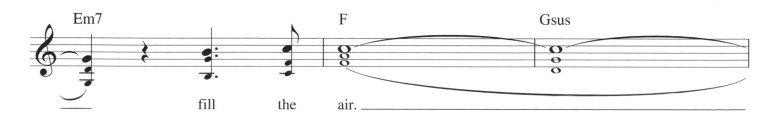

fill the air. _____

11

praise - es _____ rise to You. _____

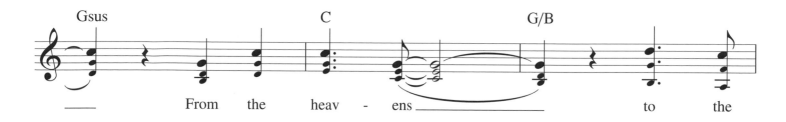

_____ From the heav - ens _____ to the

na - tions, _____ hear the sing - ing _____

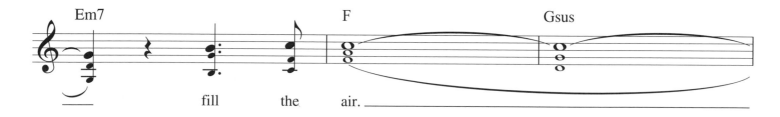

_____ fill the air. _____

**E** Bridge

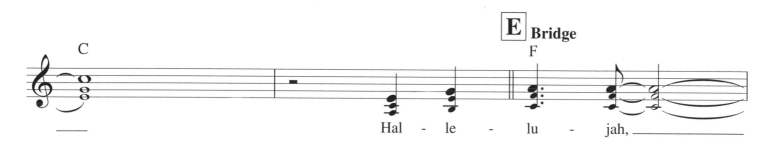

_____ Hal - le - lu - jah, _____

_____ hal - le - lu - jah, _____ hal - le -

lu - jah, _____ hal - le - lu - jah. _____

G         F         Dm7

\_\_\_ Hal - le - lu - jah, _____ hal - le -

Am         Em7         F

lu - jah, \_\_\_ hal - le - lu - jah, _____

Dm7         Gsus         G

\_\_\_ hal - le - lu - jah. _____ From the

**F** **Chorus**

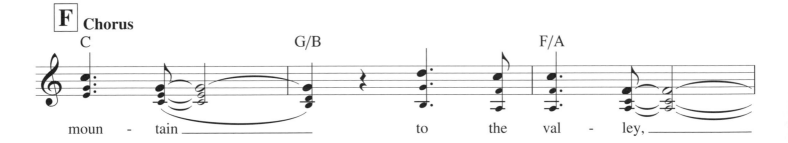

C         G/B         F/A

moun - tain _____ to the val - ley, _____

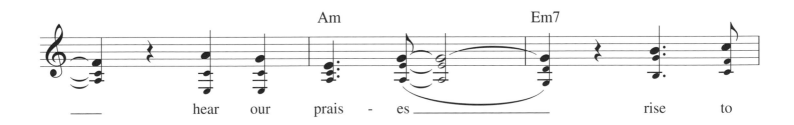

           Am         Em7

\_\_\_ hear our prais - es _____ rise to

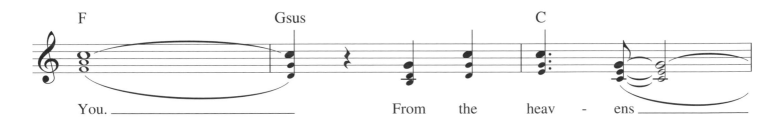

F         Gsus         C

You. _____ From the heav - ens _____

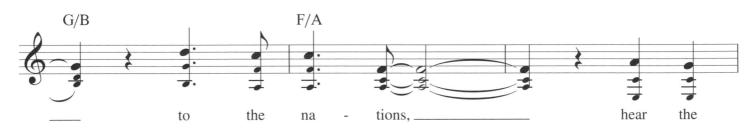

G/B         F/A

\_\_\_ to the na - tions, _____ hear the

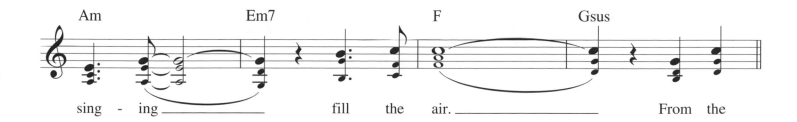

Am ......... Em7 ......... F ......... Gsus

sing - ing _____ fill the air. _____ From the

**G** **Chorus**

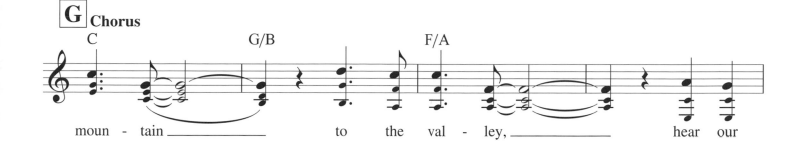

C ......... G/B ......... F/A

moun - tain _____ to the val - ley, _____ hear our

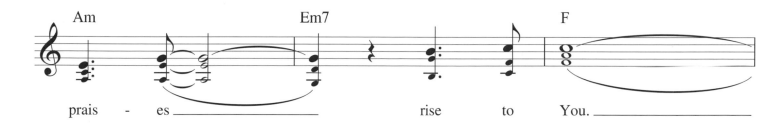

Am ......... Em7 ......... F

prais - es _____ rise to You. _____

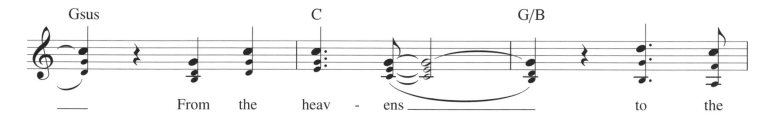

Gsus ......... C ......... G/B

_____ From the heav - ens _____ to the

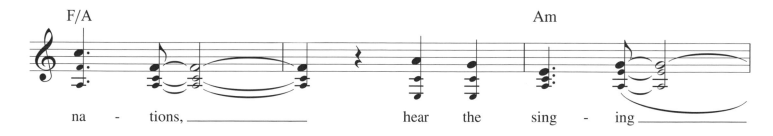

F/A ......... Am

na - tions, _____ hear the sing - ing _____

**Outro**

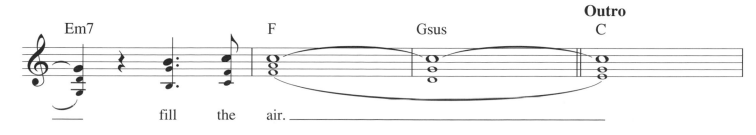

Em7 ......... F ......... Gsus ......... C

_____ fill the air. _____

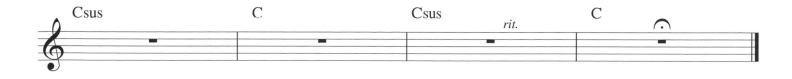

Csus ......... C ......... Csus ......... *rit.* ......... C

15

# Here I Am to Worship

**Words and Music by Tim Hughes**

7/8

**Moderately slow (♩ = 75)**
**Intro**

(Piano)

**A** **Verse 1**

Light of the world, You stepped down in-to dark - ness, o - pened my eyes, let me

see beau - ty that made this heart a - dore You,

hope of a life spent with You. Here I am to

**B** **Chorus**

wor - ship, here I am to bow down, here I am to say that You're my God.

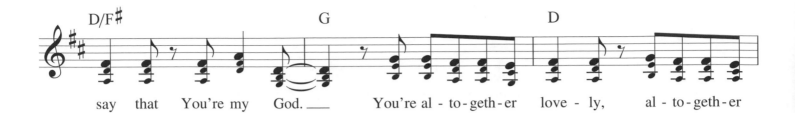

say that You're my God. ___ You're al - to - geth - er love - ly, al - to - geth - er

wor - thy, al - to - geth - er won - der - ful to me. ___ And I'll nev -

**E** Bridge

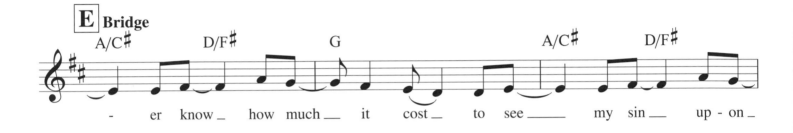

___ er know ___ how much ___ it cost ___ to see ___ my sin ___ up - on ___

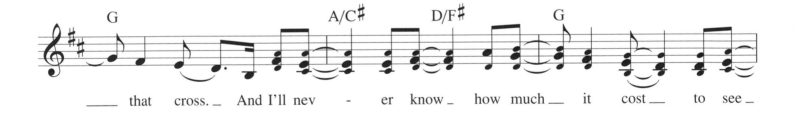

___ that cross. ___ And I'll nev - er know ___ how much ___ it cost ___ to see ___

___ my sin ___ up - on ___ that cross. ___ And here I am to

**F** Chorus

wor - ship, here I am to bow down, here I am to say that You're my God. ___

You're al - to-geth-er love - ly, al-to-geth-er wor - thy, al-to-geth-er

**G** Chorus

won - der - ful to me. ___ And here I am to wor - ship, here I am to

bow down, here I am to say that You're my God. ___ You're al - to-geth-er

love - ly, al - to-geth-er wor - thy, al - to-geth-er won - der - ful to me. ___

**H** Tag

Light of the world, You stepped

down in - to dark - ness, o - pened my eyes, let me ___ see.

# I Give You My Heart

**Words and Music by Reuben Morgan**

Moderately slow (♩ = 77)

**Intro**

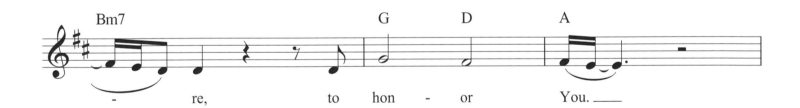

**A** **Verse**

This is my ___ de-si-

-re, to hon-or You. ___

Lord, with all ___ my heart, ___ I wor-ship You. ___

All I have ___ with-in ___ me, I

give You praise. ___ All that I ___ a - dore

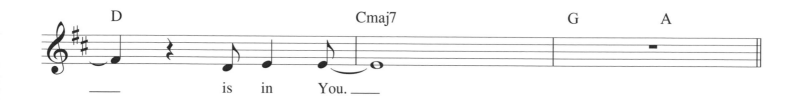

___ is in You. ___

**B** Chorus

Lord, I give You my heart, ___ I give You my ___ soul. ___ I

live for You a - lone. ___ Ev - 'ry breath that I ___ take, ___

___ ev - 'ry mo - ment I'm ___ a - wake, ___ Lord,

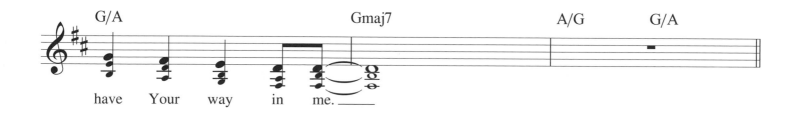

have Your way in me. ___

**C** Verse

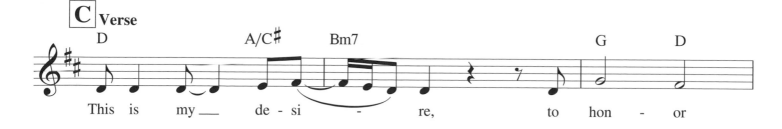

This is my ___ de - si - re, to hon - or


21

You.____  Lord, with all ___ my heart, ___  I wor-ship You. __

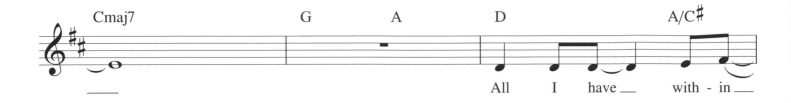

____  All  I  have ___ with - in ___

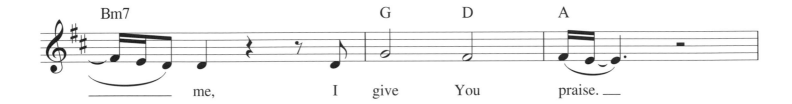

_____ me,  I  give  You  praise. __

All  that  I ___ a - dore ___  is  in  You. ___

**D** Chorus

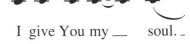

Lord,  I  give You my  heart, ___  I give You my ___ soul. _

____  I  live  for  You  a - lone. ___  Ev -'ry  breath that I ___ take, _

____  ev -'ry  mo - ment  I'm ___ a - wake, ___  Lord,

**E** **Chorus**

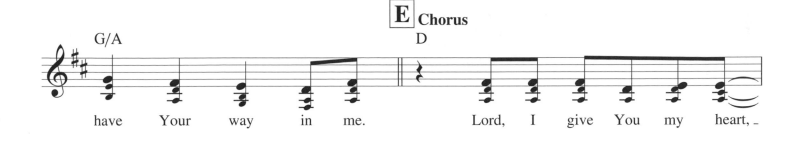

G/A                D

have   Your   way   in   me.       Lord,   I   give   You   my   heart, _

A            Em7         G/A

_____ I give You my __ soul. ___    I   live   for   You   a - lone. _

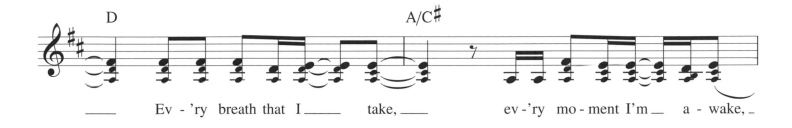

D                 A/C♯

_____ Ev - 'ry breath that I _____ take, ____   ev -'ry mo - ment I'm __ a - wake, _

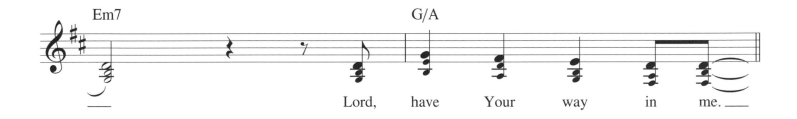

Em7                G/A

__              Lord,   have   Your   way   in   me. _

**F** **Outro**

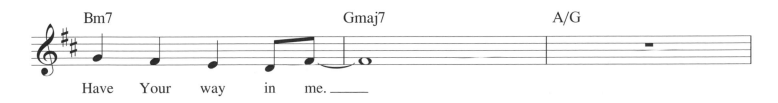

Gmaj7            A/G           F♯m7

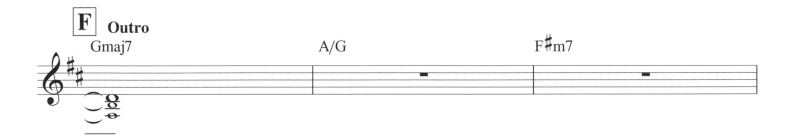

Bm7            Gmaj7         A/G

Have   Your   way   in   me. _____

F♯m7            G/A    *rit.*        D

# Let Everything That Has Breath

**Words and Music by Matt Redman**

end - less love, then sure - ly we would nev - er cease to

**D** Chorus

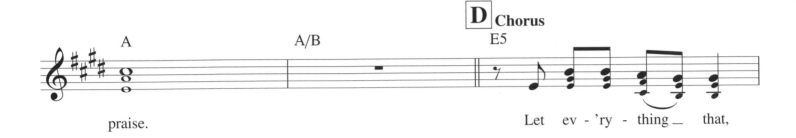

praise.                          Let ev - 'ry - thing ___ that,

ev - 'ry - thing ___ that,                    ev - 'ry - thing ___ that

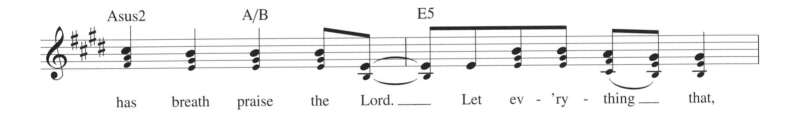

has    breath    praise    the    Lord. ___    Let    ev - 'ry - thing ___ that,

ev - 'ry - thing ___ that,                    ev - 'ry - thing ___ that

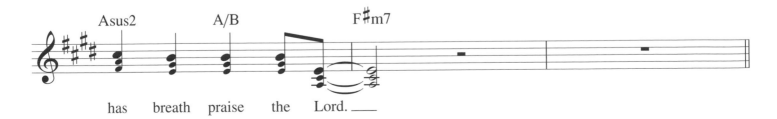

has    breath    praise    the    Lord. ___

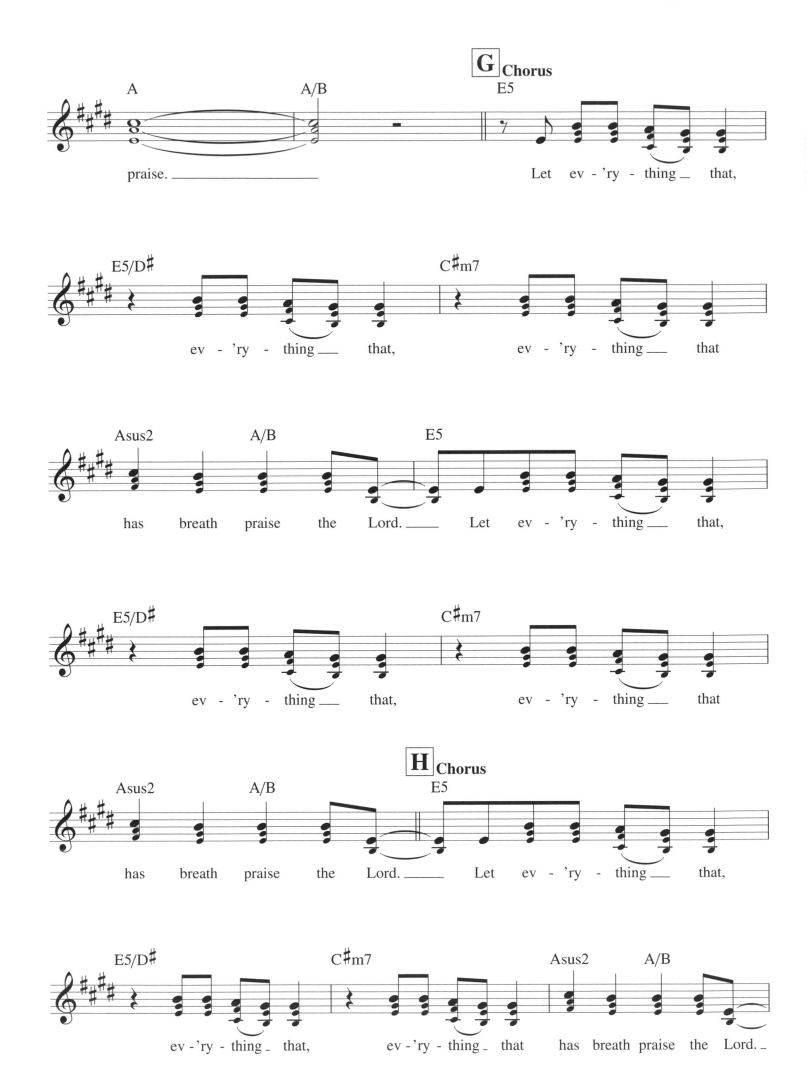

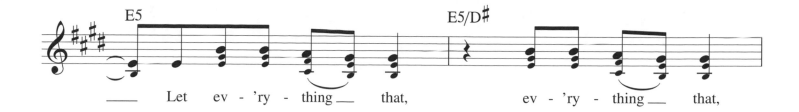

Let ev - 'ry - thing \_\_\_ that,     ev - 'ry - thing \_\_\_ that,

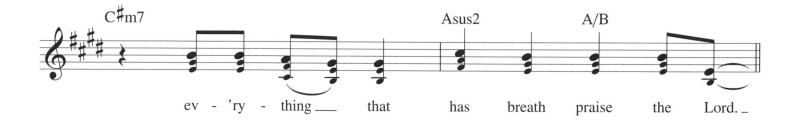

ev - 'ry - thing \_\_\_ that   has   breath   praise   the   Lord. \_

### **I** Chorus

Let ev - 'ry - thing \_\_\_ that,     ev - 'ry - thing \_\_\_ that,

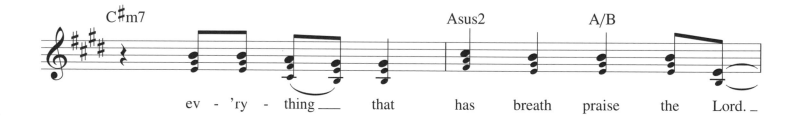

ev - 'ry - thing \_\_\_ that   has   breath   praise   the   Lord. \_

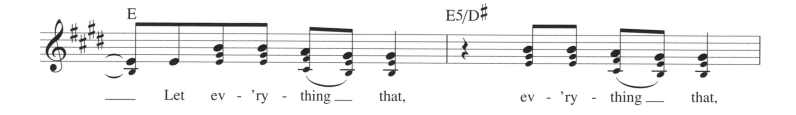

Let ev - 'ry - thing \_\_\_ that,     ev - 'ry - thing \_\_\_ that,

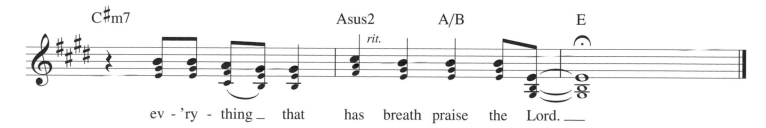

ev - 'ry - thing \_ that   has   breath   praise   the   Lord. \_\_\_

# You're Worthy of My Praise

**Words and Music by David Ruis**

**Moderately fast (♩ = 110)**

**Intro**

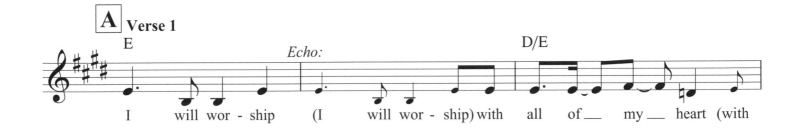

**A** **Verse 1**

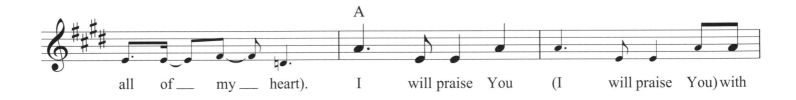

I will wor-ship (I will wor-ship) with all of __ my __ heart (with

all of __ my __ heart). I will praise You (I will praise You) with

all of __ my __ strength (all my strength). _____ I will seek You

(I will seek You) all of __ my __ days (all of __ my __ days).

I will fol - low (I will fol - low) all of __ Your __ ways

**B** Chorus

(all Your ways). _____ I will give _ You all __ my __ wor - ship,

I will give _ You all my praise. _____ You a - lone _ I

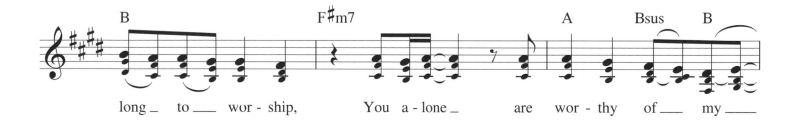

long _ to __ wor - ship, You a - lone _ are wor - thy of __ my _____

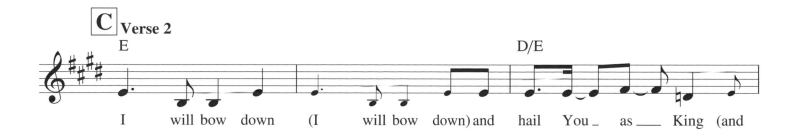

___ praise. ___

**C** Verse 2

I will bow down (I will bow down) and hail You _ as __ King (and

long _ to _ wor-ship, You a-lone _ are wor-thy of _ my praise. _

**E** **Chorus**

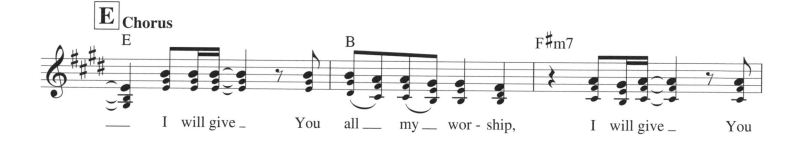

_ I will give _ You all _ my _ wor-ship, I will give _ You

all my praise. _____ You a-lone _ I long _ to _ wor-ship,

You a-lone _ are wor-thy of _ my _ praise. _____

**F** **Tag**

_ You're wor-thy of _ my _ praise. _____

_ You're wor-thy of _ my _ praise.

# You Alone

**Words and Music by Jack Parker and David Crowder**

**With a lilt (♩. = ca. 50)**

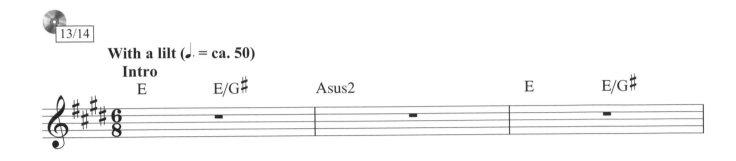

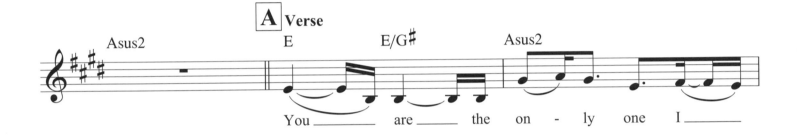

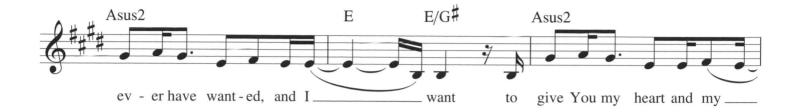

ev - er have want - ed, and I _____ want to give You my heart and my _____

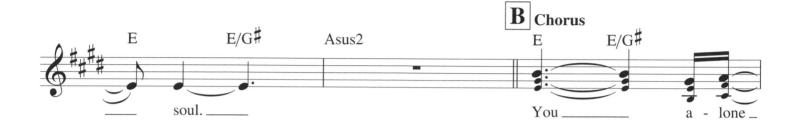

_____ soul. _____

**B** Chorus

You _____ a - lone _

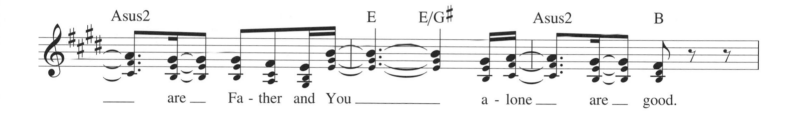

_____ are _ Fa - ther and You _____ a - lone _ are _ good.

You _____ a - lone _ are _ Sav - ior and You _____ a - lone _

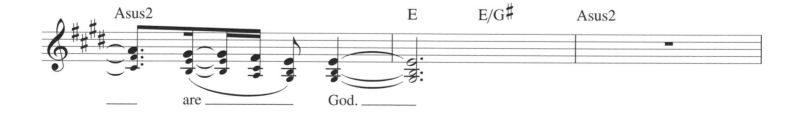

_____ are _____ God. _____

**C** Verse

You _____ are _____ the

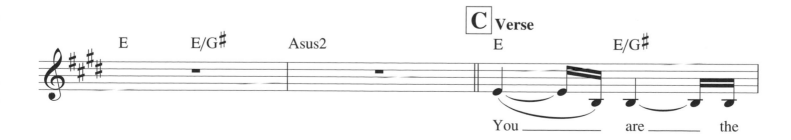

on - ly one I _____ need, _____ I bow all of me at Your \_\_\_\_

feet, _____ I wor - ship You a - lone. \_\_\_\_

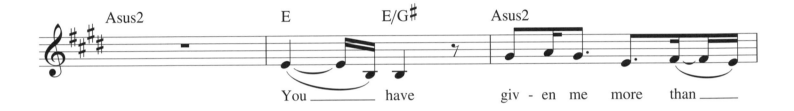

You _____ have giv - en me more than \_\_\_\_\_

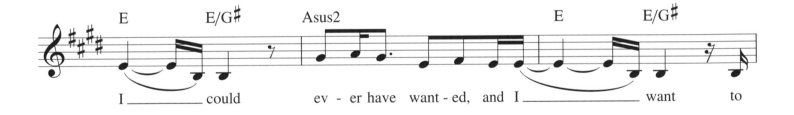

I _____ could ev - er have want - ed, and I _____ want to

give You my heart and my _____ soul. \_\_\_\_

**D** Chorus

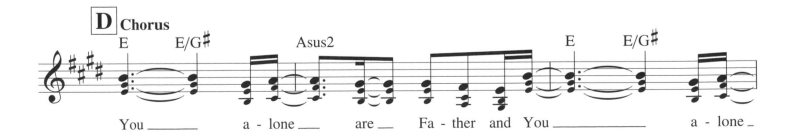

You _____ a - lone \_\_\_ are \_\_ Fa - ther and You _____ a - lone \_\_

are good. You a-lone are Sav-ior and You

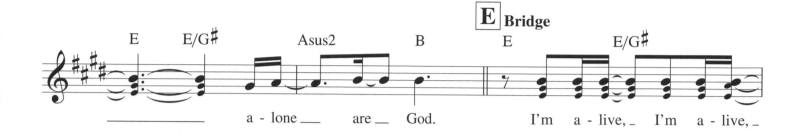

**E Bridge**

a-lone are God. I'm a-live, I'm a-live,

I'm a-live, I'm a-live. I'm a-live, I'm a-live,

I'm a-live, I'm a-live. I'm a-live, I'm a-live,

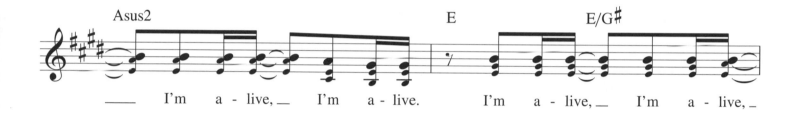

I'm a-live, I'm a-live. I'm a-live, I'm a-live.

**F Chorus**

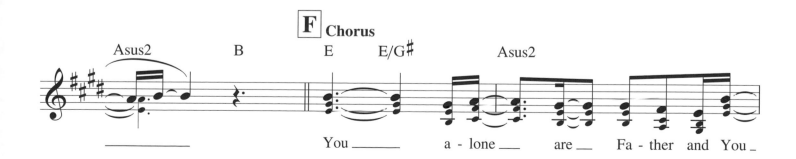

You a-lone are Fa-ther and You

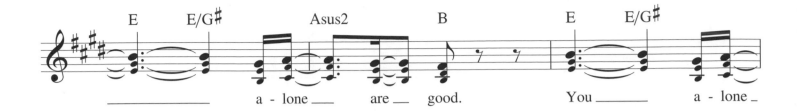

a - lone ___ are ___ good. You ___ a - lone ___

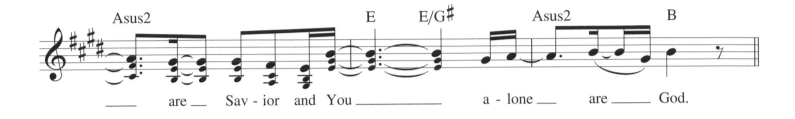

___ are ___ Sav - ior and You ___ a - lone ___ are ___ God.

### G Chorus

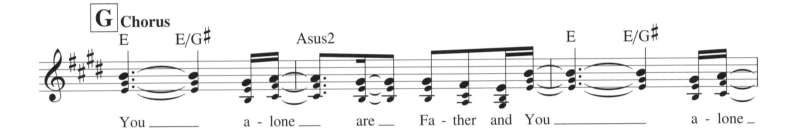

You ___ a - lone ___ are ___ Fa - ther and You ___ a - lone ___

___ are ___ good. You ___ a - lone ___ are ___ Sav - ior and You ___

**Outro**

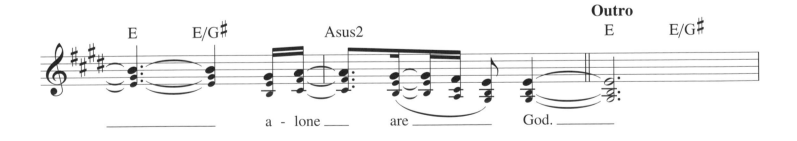

___ a - lone ___ are ___ God.

*slight rit.*

# COME, NOW IS THE TIME TO WORSHIP

BRIAN DOERKSEN

Key of **D Major**, 4/4

**INTRO:**

D   G/D D   G/D

**VERSE:**

D                      G/D    D
Come, now is the time to wor  -  ship

A                    Em7    D/F♯   G
Come, now is the time to give     your   heart

D                      G/D    D
Come, just as you are, to wor  -  ship

A                    Em7 D/F♯    G
Come, just as you are, before   your   God

D
Come

**CHORUS:**

G                            D
One day ev'ry tongue will confess You are God

G                    D
One day ev'ry knee will bow

G                        Bm
Still, the greatest treasure remains for those

     Em7           Asus     A
Who gladly choose You now

**(REPEAT VERSE)**

**(REPEAT CHORUS 2X)**

**(REPEAT VERSE)**

**OUTRO:**

   D   G/D D   G/D  D (hold)
(Come)    Come    Come

# GIVE US CLEAN HANDS

CHARLIE HALL

Key of **G Major, 4/4**

### INTRO:

G   D   G/B C   G

### VERSE:

G                           D                           G/B
   We bow our hearts, we bend our knees
C                                   G
   O Spirit, come make us humble
G                           D                           G/B
   We turn our eyes from evil things
C
   O Lord, we cast down our idols

### CHORUS:

C/D                 G                           D
Give us clean hands, give us pure hearts
      Em             D             G
Let us not lift our souls to another
           G                           D
Give us clean hands, give us pure hearts
      Em             D             G
Let us not lift our souls to another
           G                           D
And God, let us be a generation that seeks
           Em       D       G
That seeks Your face, O God of Jacob
           G                           D
And God, let us be a generation that seeks
          Em     D     Csus2 (2 bars)
That seeks Your face, O God of Jacob

### (REPEAT VERSE & CHORUS)

### TAG:

G                           D                           G/B
   We bow our hearts, we bend our knees
C                                       G (hold)
   O Spirit, come make us humble

# HEAR OUR PRAISES

REUBEN MORGAN

Key of **C Major, 4/4**

## INTRO:

C   Csus   C   Csus

## VERSE 1:

C         Csus         C   G/B
     May our homes be filled with dancing

Am        F        Gsus   G
     May our streets be filled with joy

C         Csus         C   G/B
     May injustice bow to Jesus

Am        F        Gsus   G
     As the people turn to pray

## CHORUS:

        C   G/B      F/A
From the mountain    to the valley

        Am   Em7      F   Gsus
Hear our praises     rise to You

        C   G/B      F/A
From the heavens    to the nations

        Am   Em7      F   Gsus
Hear the singing     fill the air

## (REPEAT INTRO)

## VERSE 2:

C         Csus         C   G/B
     May our light shine in the darkness

Am        F        Gsus   G
     As we walk before the cross

C         Csus         C   G/B
     May Your glory fill the whole earth

Am        F        Gsus   G
     As the water o'er the seas

## (REPEAT CHORUS)

## TRANSITION TO BRIDGE:

C (2 bars)

## BRIDGE (2X):

     F    Dm7       Am   Em7
Hallelujah,      hallelujah

     F    Dm7       Gsus    G
Hallelujah,      hallelujah

## (REPEAT CHORUS 2X)

## OUTRO:

C   Csus   C   Csus   C (hold)

# HERE I AM TO WORSHIP

TIM HUGHES

Key of **D Major**, 4/4

### INTRO:

D    A    Em7    D    A    G

### VERSE 1:

D          A              Em7
Light of the world, You stepped down into darkness

D          A         G
Opened my eyes, let me see

D          A             Em7
Beauty that made this heart adore You

D          A           G (2 bars)
Hope of a life spent with You

### CHORUS:

                D                 A
Here I am to worship, here I am to bow down

             D/F♯            G
Here I am to say that You're my God

                   D            A
You're altogether lovely, altogether worthy

             D/F♯      G
Altogether wonderful to me

### VERSE 2:

D          A             Em7
King of all days, oh, so highly exalted

D          A       G
Glorious in heaven above

D          A           Em7
Humbly You came to the earth You created

D          A           G (1 bar)
All for love's sake became poor

### (REPEAT CHORUS)

### BRIDGE (2X):

       A/C♯     D/F♯      G
And I'll never know   how much it cost

   A/C♯     D/F♯  G
To see my sin    upon that cross

### (REPEAT CHORUS 2X)

### TAG:

D          A              Em7
Light of the world, You stepped down into darkness

D          A         G (hold)
Opened my eyes, let me see

# I GIVE YOU MY HEART

REUBEN MORGAN

---

Key of **D Major, 4/4**

**INTRO:**

Gmaj7  A/G  F#m7  Bm7
Gmaj7  A/G  F#m7  G/A

**VERSE:**

D      A/C# Bm7
This is my de - sire

  G   D A
To hon - or You

Bm7      A/C#  D
Lord, with all  my  heart

      Cmaj7    G  A
I worship You

D      A/C#  Bm7
All I have with - in me

  G   D   A
I give You praise

Bm7  A/C#   D
All that I a - dore

    Cmaj7    G  A
Is in You

**CHORUS:**

D               A
Lord, I give You my heart

            Em7
I give You my soul

 G/A
I live for You alone

D          A/C#
Ev'ry breath that I take

            Em7
Ev'ry moment I'm awake

   G/A            (Gmaj7  A/G  G/A)
Lord, have Your way in me

**(REPEAT VERSE)**

**(REPEAT CHORUS 2X)**

**OUTRO:**

Gmaj7  A/G  F#m7  Bm7
Gmaj7  A/G  F#m7  G/A  D (hold)

# LET EVERYTHING THAT HAS BREATH

MATT REDMAN

Key of **E Major**, 4/4

### INTRO:

E5    E5/D♯    C♯m7    Asus2  A/B

E5    E5/D♯    C♯m7    Asus2  A/B    F♯m7 (2 bars)

### CHORUS:

E5               E5/D♯
Let everything that, everything that

C♯m7      Asus2     A/B
Everything that has breath praise the Lord

E5               E5/D♯
Let everything that, everything that

C♯m7      Asus2     A/B    F♯m7 (2 bars)
Everything that has breath praise the Lord

### VERSE 1:

E5
Praise You in the morning

E5/D♯
Praise You in the evening

C♯m7                       Asus2
Praise You when I'm young and when I'm old

E5
Praise You when I'm laughing

E5/D♯
Praise You when I'm grieving

C♯m7          Asus2
Praise You ev'ry season of the soul

### PRE-CHORUS 1:

 F♯m7         E/G♯
If we could see how much You're worth

   F♯m7         E/G♯
Your pow'r, Your might, Your endless love

   F♯m7     E/G♯     A  A/B
Then surely we would never cease to praise

### (REPEAT CHORUS)

### VERSE 2:

E5
Praise You in the heavens

E5/D♯
Joining with the angels

C♯m7                Asus2
Praising You forever and a day

E5
Praise You on the earth now

E5/D♯
Joining with creation

C♯m7                Asus2
Calling all the nations to Your praise

### PRE-CHORUS 2:

 F♯m7         E/G♯
If they could see how much You're worth

   F♯m7         E/G♯
Your pow'r, Your might, Your endless love

   F♯m7     E/G♯     A  A/B
Then surely they would never cease to praise

### (REPEAT CHORUS 3X)

### END ON E

# YOU ALONE

JACK PARKER and DAVID CROWDER

Key of **E Major**, 6/8

**INTRO:**

E  E/G♯  Asus2

E  E/G♯  Asus2

**VERSE:**

E     E/G♯     Asus2
You   are   the only one I

E     E/G♯     Asus2
Need,  I  bow all of me at Your

E     E/G♯  Asus2       E  E/G♯  Asus2
Feet,   I   worship You alone

E     E/G♯     Asus2
You   have   given me more than

E  E/G♯     Asus2
I  could   ever have wanted, and

E  E/G♯     Asus2               E  E/G♯  Asus2
I  want   to give You my heart and my soul

**CHORUS:**

E     E/G♯     Asus2
You       alone are Father

      E  E/G♯  Asus2      B
And You      alone are good

E     E/G♯     Asus2
You       alone are Savior

      E  E/G♯  Asus2   (B)
And You       alone are God

**INTERLUDE:**

E  E/G♯  Asus2

E  E/G♯  Asus2

**(REPEAT VERSE & CHORUS)**

**BRIDGE:**

E     E/G♯     Asus2
I'm alive, I'm alive, I'm alive, I'm alive

E     E/G♯     Asus2
I'm alive, I'm alive, I'm alive, I'm alive

E     E/G♯     Asus2
I'm alive, I'm alive, I'm alive, I'm alive

E  E/G♯     Asus2  B
I'm alive, I'm alive

**(REPEAT CHORUS 2X)**

**OUTRO:**

E  E/G♯  Asus2

E  E/G♯  Asus2  E (hold)

# YOU'RE WORTHY OF MY PRAISE

DAVID RUIS

Key of **E Major**, 4/4

**INTRO:**

E    D/E

**VERSE 1:**

E           *Echo:*
I will worship (*I will worship*)

    D/E
With all of my heart (*with all of my heart*)

A
I will praise You (*I will praise You*)

     E            F#m7    Bsus B
With all of my strength (*all my strength*)

E
I will seek You (*I will seek You*)

D/E
All of my days (*all of my days*)

A
I will follow (*I will follow*)

E          F#m7    Bsus B
All of Your ways (*all Your ways*)

**CHORUS:**

E             B
I will give You all my worship

F#m7       A     Bsus B
I will give You all my praise

E           B
You alone I long to worship

F#m7        A   Bsus B   E   D/E
You alone are worthy of    my praise

**VERSE 2:**

E
I will bow down (*I will bow down*)

    D/E
And hail You as King (*and hail You as King*)

A
I will serve You (*I will serve You*)

         E       F#m7    Bsus B
Give You ev'rything (*give You ev'rything*)

E
I will lift up (*I will lift up*)

    D/E
My eyes to Your throne (*my eyes to Your throne*)

A
I will trust You (*I will trust You*)

E          F#m7    Bsus B
Trust You alone (*trust in You alone*)

**(REPEAT CHORUS 2X)**

**TAG:**

       A   Bsus B   E   D/E
You're worthy of   my praise

       A   Bsus B   E (hold)
You're worthy of   my praise

# Pro Vocal® Series
## SONGBOOK & SOUND-ALIKE CD
### SING 8 GREAT SONGS
### WITH A PROFESSIONAL BAND

Whether you're a karaoke singer or an auditioning professional, the Pro Vocal® series is for you! Unlike most karaoke packs, each book in the Pro Vocal Series contains the lyrics, melody, and chord symbols for eight hit songs. The CD contains demos for listening, and separate backing tracks so you can sing along. The CD is playable on any CD player, but it is also enhanced so PC and Mac computer users can adjust the recording to any pitch without changing the tempo! Perfect for home rehearsal, parties, auditions, corporate events, and gigs without a backup band.

## WOMEN'S EDITIONS

| | | |
|---|---|---|
| 00740409 | **1. Broadway Standards** | $14.95 |
| 00740249 | **2. Jazz Standards** | $14.95 |
| 00740246 | **3. Contemporary Hits** | $14.95 |
| 00740277 | **4. '80s Gold** | $12.95 |
| 00740299 | **5. Christmas Standards** | $15.95 |
| 00740281 | **6. Disco Fever** | $12.95 |
| 00740279 | **7. R&B Super Hits** | $12.95 |
| 00740309 | **8. Wedding Gems** | $12.95 |
| 00740409 | **9. Broadway Standards** | $14.95 |
| 00740348 | **10. Andrew Lloyd Webber** | $14.95 |
| 00740344 | **11. Disney's Best** | $14.95 |
| 00740378 | **12. Ella Fitzgerald** | $14.95 |
| 00740350 | **14. Musicals of Boublil & Schönberg** | $14.95 |
| 00740377 | **15. Kelly Clarkson** | $14.95 |
| 00740377 | **16. Disney Favorites** | $14.95 |
| 00740353 | **17. Jazz Ballads** | $12.95 |
| 00740376 | **18. Jazz Vocal Standards** | $14.95 |
| 00740375 | **20. Hannah Montana** | $16.95 |
| 00740354 | **21. Jazz Favorites** | $12.95 |
| 00740374 | **22. Patsy Cline** | $14.95 |
| 00740369 | **23. Grease** | $14.95 |
| 00740367 | **25. ABBA** | $14.95 |
| 00740365 | **26. Movie Songs** | $14.95 |
| 00740360 | **28. High School Musical 1 & 2** | $14.95 |
| 00740363 | **29. Torch Songs** | $14.95 |
| 00740379 | **30. Hairspray** | $14.95 |
| 00740380 | **31. Top Hits** | $14.95 |
| 00740384 | **32. Hits of the '70s** | $14.95 |
| 00740388 | **33. Billie Holiday** | $14.95 |
| 00740389 | **34. The Sound of Music** | $14.95 |
| 00740390 | **35. Contemporary Christian** | $14.95 |
| 00740392 | **36. Wicked** | $14.95 |
| 00740393 | **37. More Hannah Montana** | $14.95 |
| 00740394 | **38. Miley Cyrus** | $14.95 |
| 00740396 | **39. Christmas Hits** | $15.95 |
| 00740410 | **40. Broadway Classics** | $14.95 |
| 00740415 | **41. Broadway Favorites** | $14.95 |
| 00740416 | **42. Great Standards You Can Sing** | $14.95 |
| 00740417 | **43. Singable Standards** | $14.95 |
| 00740418 | **44. Favorite Standards** | $14.95 |
| 00740419 | **45. Sing Broadway** | $14.95 |
| 00740420 | **46. More Standards** | $14.95 |
| 00740421 | **47. Timeless Hits** | $14.95 |
| 00740422 | **48. Easygoing R&B** | $14.95 |

## MEN'S EDITIONS

| | | |
|---|---|---|
| 00740248 | **1. Broadway Songs** | $14.95 |
| 00740250 | **2. Jazz Standards** | $14.95 |
| 00740251 | **3. Contemporary Hits** | $14.95 |
| 00740278 | **4. '80s Gold** | $12.95 |
| 00740298 | **5. Christmas Standards** | $15.95 |
| 00740280 | **6. R&B Super Hits** | $12.95 |
| 00740282 | **7. Disco Fever** | $12.95 |
| 00740310 | **8. Wedding Gems** | $12.95 |
| 00740411 | **9. Broadway Greats** | $14.95 |
| 00740333 | **10. Elvis Presley – Volume 1** | $14.95 |
| 00740349 | **11. Andrew Lloyd Webber** | $14.95 |
| 00740345 | **12. Disney's Best** | $14.95 |
| 00740347 | **13. Frank Sinatra Classics** | $14.95 |
| 00740334 | **14. Lennon & McCartney** | $14.95 |
| 00740335 | **15. Elvis Presley – Volume 2** | $14.95 |
| 00740343 | **17. Disney Favorites** | $14.95 |
| 00740351 | **18. Musicals of Boublil & Schönberg** | $14.95 |
| 00740346 | **20. Frank Sinatra Standards** | $14.95 |
| 00740362 | **27. Michael Bublé** | $14.95 |
| 00740361 | **28. High School Musical 1 & 2** | $14.95 |
| 00740364 | **29. Torch Songs** | $14.95 |
| 00740366 | **30. Movie Songs** | $14.95 |
| 00740368 | **31. Hip Hop Hits** | $14.95 |
| 00740370 | **32. Grease** | $14.95 |
| 00740371 | **33. Josh Groban** | $14.95 |
| 00740373 | **34. Billy Joel** | $17.95 |
| 00740381 | **35. Hits of the '50s** | $14.95 |
| 00740382 | **36. Hits of the '60s** | $14.95 |
| 00740383 | **37. Hits of the '70s** | $14.95 |
| 00740385 | **38. Motown** | $14.95 |
| 00740386 | **39. Hank Williams** | $14.95 |
| 00740387 | **40. Neil Diamond** | $14.95 |
| 00740391 | **41. Contemporary Christian** | $14.95 |
| 00740397 | **42. Christmas Hits** | $15.95 |
| 00740399 | **43. Ray** | $14.95 |
| 00740400 | **44. The Rat Pack Hits** | $14.95 |
| 00740401 | **45. Songs in the Style of Nat "King" Cole** | $14.95 |
| 00740402 | **46. At the Lounge** | $14.95 |
| 00740403 | **47. The Big Band Singer** | $14.95 |
| 00740404 | **48. Jazz Cabaret Songs** | $14.95 |
| 00740405 | **49. Cabaret Songs** | $14.95 |
| 00740406 | **50. Big Band Standards** | $14.95 |
| 00740412 | **51. Broadway's Best** | $14.95 |

## MIXED EDITIONS

*These editions feature songs for both male and female voices.*

| | | |
|---|---|---|
| 00740311 | **1. Wedding Duets** | $12.95 |
| 00740398 | **2. Enchanted** | $14.95 |
| 00740407 | **3. Rent** | $14.95 |
| 00740408 | **4. Broadway Favorites** | $14.95 |
| 00740413 | **5. South Pacific** | $14.95 |
| 00740414 | **6. High School Musical 3** | $14.95 |

FOR MORE INFORMATION, SEE YOUR LOCAL MUSIC DEALER,
OR WRITE TO:

## HAL•LEONARD® CORPORATION
7777 W. BLUEMOUND RD. P.O. BOX 13819 MILWAUKEE, WI 53213

**Visit Hal Leonard online at www.halleonard.com**

Prices, contents, & availability subject to change without notice.
Disney charaters and artwork © Disney Enterprises, Inc.

1008

# Worship Band Play-Along

The **Worship Band Play-Along** series is a flexible tool for worship leaders and bands. Each volume offers five separate, correlated book/CD packs: Guitar, Keyboard, Bass, Drumset, and Vocal. Bands can use the printed music and chord charts to play live together, and members can rehearse at home with the CD tracks. Worship leaders without a band can play/sing along with the CD for a fuller sound. The eight songs in each volume follow a similar theme for easy set selection, and the straightforward arrangements are perfect for bands of any level.

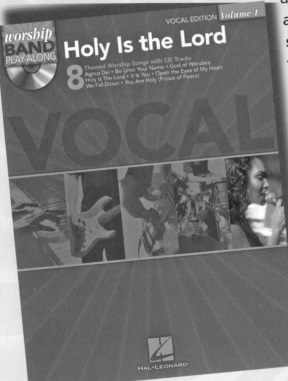

## 1. Holy Is the Lord

Includes: Agnus Dei • Be Unto Your Name • God of Wonders • Holy Is the Lord • It Is You • Open the Eyes of My Heart • We Fall Down • You Are Holy (Prince of Peace).

| | | |
|---|---|---|
| 08740302 | Vocal | $12.95 |
| 08740333 | Keyboard | $12.95 |
| 08740334 | Guitar | $12.95 |
| 08740335 | Bass | $12.95 |
| 08740336 | Drumset | $12.95 |

## COMING SOON!

## 4. He Is Exalted

Includes: Beautiful One • God of All • He Is Exalted • In Christ Alone • Lord Most High • Lord, Reign in Me • We Want to See Jesus Lifted High • Worthy Is the Lamb.

| | | |
|---|---|---|
| 08740646 | Vocal | $12.95 |
| 08740651 | Keyboard | $12.95 |
| 08740712 | Guitar | $12.95 |
| 08740741 | Bass | $12.95 |
| 08745665 | Drumset | $12.95 |

## 2. Here I Am to Worship

Includes: Come, Now Is the Time to Worship • Give Us Clean Hands • Hear Our Praises • Here I Am to Worship • I Give You My Heart • Let Everything That Has Breath • You Alone • You're Worthy of My Praise.

| | | |
|---|---|---|
| 08740337 | Vocal | $12.95 |
| 08740338 | Keyboard | $12.95 |
| 08740409 | Guitar | $12.95 |
| 08740441 | Bass | $12.95 |
| 08740444 | Drumset | $12.95 |

## 3. How Great Is Our God

Includes: Above All • Beautiful Savior (All My Days) • Days of Elijah • How Great Is Our God • Let My Words Be Few (I'll Stand in Awe of You) • No One Like You • Wonderful Maker • Yesterday, Today and Forever.

| | | |
|---|---|---|
| 08740540 | Vocal | $12.95 |
| 08740571 | Keyboard | $12.95 |
| 08740572 | Guitar | $12.95 |
| 08740608 | Bass | $12.95 |
| 08740635 | Drumset | $12.95 |

FOR MORE INFORMATION, SEE YOUR LOCAL MUSIC DEALER, OR WRITE TO:

# HAL•LEONARD® CORPORATION

7777 W. BLUEMOUND RD. P.O. BOX 13819 MILWAUKEE, WI 53213

**www.halleonard.com**

Prices, contents, and availability subject to change without notice.